ANIMALS IN DANGER

Written by Ian Gray, Vassili Papastavrou,
Malcolm Penny, Ian Redmond,
Helen Riley and Gillian Standring

WORLD INTERNATIONAL PUBLISHING LIMITED
MANCHESTER

Copyright © 1990, 1991 Wayland (Publishers) Limited.
This edition published in Great Britain in 1991 by
World International Publishing Limited in association with
Wayland (Publishers) Limited. All rights reserved.
World International Publishing Limited, an Egmont Company,
Egmont House, PO Box 111, Great Ducie Street, Manchester M60 3BL.
Printed in Singapore.
ISBN 0 7498 0439 4

No part of this publication may be reproduced, stored in a retrieval system, or transmitted, in any form or by any means, electronic, mechanical, photocopying, recording or otherwise, without the prior permission of the publishers.

Author acknowledgements
Written by Ian Gray (pages 22–27), Vassili Papastavrou (pages 34–39), Malcolm Penny (pages 28–33 and 48–53), Ian Redmond (pages 15–21 and 40–47), Helen Riley (pages 8–14) and Gillian Standring (pages 54–59).

Picture acknowledgements
Bryan and Cherry Alexander 32, 34; Ardier London 37 (Francois Gohier); Bruce Coleman Ltd 36 (Jeff Foott); Bruce Coleman/M P Price 12 bottom; Steve Dawson 38; FOVEA 48 right (Jung-Kwan Chi); Robert Harding Photo Library 49; Okapia 54 (Christine Grzimek); Planet Earth Pictures 55 top (Franz Camenzind); Rex Features Ltd 56, 58 bottom; Survival Anglia 53 (Jen and Des Bartlett); WWF/Tim Rautert 55 bottom, 58 top; ZEFA 57 (Dr P Thiele). All remaining photographs from Oxford Scientific Films by the following photographers: R A Acharya 10; Rafi Ben-Shahar 13; G I Bernard 45; Mike Birkhead 22; Stanley Breedon 9, 11, 46 top; Margot Conte 33 left; Carol Farneti 41; Mickey Gibson/Animals Animals 8; Roger de la Harpe 48 left; Philippe Henry 26 bottom, 29 top; Frank Huber 31; Richard Kolar 29 bottom; Lon E Lauber 23, 25, 27; Michael Leach 26 top, 30 bottom; Tony Martin 35; Richard Packwood 42, 47, 51; Vassili Papastavrou 39; Tony and Sheila Phelps 24; Andrew Plumptre 20; Ian Redmond 15, 16, 17, 18, 19, 40 bottom, 43; Eric Reisinger 52; Alan Root/Okapia 50; Edwin Sadd 40 top; Stouffer Productions Ltd 30 top; Tom Ulrich 33 right; Belinda Wright 12 top, 14. The artwork on pages 21, 24 and 44 is by John Yates.

CONTENTS

Why are tigers so rare?	8
Gorillas in danger	15
Birds in danger	22
Bears in danger	28
Whales in danger	34
Elephants in danger	40
Why are rhinos at risk?	48
Why are pandas so rare?	54
Glossary	60
Index	61

Why are tigers so rare?

Animals in Danger

Thousands of years ago in Asia, humans and tigers hunted the same animals for food. People began to hunt tigers because of this. At first tigers were killed with spears or bows and arrows. The men hunting them either went on foot or rode elephants or horses. But the tigers knew their territories so well that they could escape easily.

When guns were invented, killing tigers became much easier. Tiger-hunting became a sport for rich people who liked to display the tigers' beautiful skins in their homes.

Sumatran tigers have become very rare because of hunting. Today only a few hundred survive in the wild.

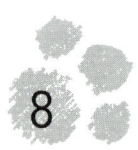

Animals in Danger

These people are stuffing the skins of dead tigers and leopards. Today in most countries it is against the law to sell the skins of rare animals like tigers. However, some people still trap tigers to sell their skins.

Many people travelled from Europe to India to shoot tigers. At the start of a hunt, local people or servants rounded up all the tigers in an area. The tigers were then driven towards the place where the hunters waited with their guns. Up to a hundred tigers could be shot on one hunting trip. As more and more tigers were shot, they became rare.

Right *Often tigers appear on religious ornaments like this Hindu sculpture.*

Animals in Danger

Tigers have also become rare because their forest homes have been destroyed. Over the past hundred years or so, the number of people living in Asia has grown greatly. The forests where the tigers live have been cut down to make way for farms and villages. In South-east Asia large areas of tropical forest have been felled because the wood from tropical trees is very valuable.

A tiger in the lush vegetation of an Asian forest.

Animals in Danger

As the forests disappeared, the tigers and other animals that lived in them had less room to live. Often they moved to small areas of untouched forest. But even there, the tigers were not safe. People still shot or poisoned tigers because they thought they were pests. This is because tigers living at the edges of natural forests will sometimes kill domestic animals like cattle or donkeys. Also, some tigers that are too old or too ill to catch wild animals may learn to attack and eat people.

As hunting and forest destruction continued, tigers became rarer and rarer. For a while, it looked as though they would very soon become extinct.

These Indian forests are being cleared to make way for tea plantations. Tigers need forests like these.

Animals in Danger

So far, the campaign to save tigers from extinction has been a great success. Today scientists think that there are twice as many tigers living in the reserves as there were twenty years ago.

Does this mean that tigers are no longer in danger? Unfortunately not. More and more people are living in the countries where tigers are found. All these extra people

Tigers need plenty of space to enjoy their active life.

need space to live and grow food. So the natural forests are still being cleared and this is bad news for tigers. Soon the only areas left for them may be the reserves.

Tigers need plenty of space. Many of the reserves are too small for a large number of tigers. Where there is only a small tiger population, the animals are in danger of becoming inbred. This happens when animals mate with a close relative, and they have weak babies.

This wild Indian tigress has been captured and fitted with a radio collar. The collar gives out radio signals, so that scientists can keep track of the tiger's movements.

Animals in Danger

If there are too few tigers in a reserve, other tigers could be brought in from elsewhere. Wildlife workers may do this in future.

There are also problems if the tiger population of a reserve grows too much. Then the reserve becomes overcrowded and tigers may spill out on to nearby farmland. Here they will eat the farmer's cattle. Tigers also sometimes attack people. So any tigers that make a nuisance of themselves must be moved elsewhere.

These Siberian tiger cubs were born in a zoo in Israel. In the future, tigers bred in zoos may be brought into areas where wild tigers have died out.

Animals in Danger

Tigers will only be really safe if the people who live near them help to save them. A poor Asian farmer will not want to save tigers if a tiger has just eaten his only cow. But sometimes tigers can help farmers. If tigers disappear, the animals they eat may grow in numbers. In some areas of India and Indonesia there are too many deer and wild boar. They like to eat the farmer's crops. This did not happen when there were tigers to keep their numbers down.

Operation Tiger has helped other animals, too. The tiger reserves protect large areas of tropical forest, where many rare plants and animals live.

*Some people think tigers are fierce killers (**left**). Others say they are beautiful majestic animals (**right**). What do you think of tigers?*

Animals in Danger

Gorillas are at risk for different reasons in different parts of Africa. By far the most serious problem is that their **habitat** is being destroyed. The trees of the rainforest are cut down by **timber companies** and land is cleared so that people can grow crops. Like many other creatures that live in the rainforest, the gorillas cannot survive if they lose their forest home. In many places, groups of gorillas have been cut off from one another. Their home ranges used to be covered by the vast forests. But now the forests have become small pockets of trees, surrounded by farms.

Above When rainforests are chopped down, gorillas are one of the many species that suffer.

Below Every patch of land that is cleared for crops means less room for wild animals.

Gorillas in danger

Animals in Danger

Where people grow bananas in gorilla country, the gorillas are seen as pests. Not only do they eat the bananas, they pull apart the trees and eat the soft pith inside them. This kills the trees, and may mean that the farmer and his family will go hungry. A farmer might shoot gorillas that are eating his crops, but we can hardly blame the farmer for protecting his family's food supply.

A mountain gorilla looks over his forest home. His home range used to get smaller every year; now the area is protected.

Animals in Danger

The gorillas themselves are eaten in parts of west and central Africa. This is another reason why the gorillas in those areas are being wiped out. Until recently, very few local hunters could afford a gun. The killing of a gorilla was a big event and did not happen very often. Now, it is much easier to get hold of a shot-gun, or even a machine gun. This means that more people are hunting gorillas for food than before. Many of them take the gorilla meat to the towns to sell. In some areas, more gorillas are being shot than are born each year and numbers are falling.

This man has been caught killing protected animals in a national park in Rwanda. He may be sent to prison.

Animals in Danger

Gorilla fingers can be bought at this traditional medicine stall in Congo. They are made into magic charms that their owners believe will give them the strength of a gorilla.

Gorillas are protected by the law in every country that they live in. The trouble is that most governments are unable to make sure that people obey the law. Many people living in villages deep in the forest do not even know that there are any laws against killing gorillas.

Sometimes the problem is caused by old traditions. In Congo, for example, many people believe that a bit of dried gorilla finger can be made into a **charm** to give strength to the owner. So gorilla hands and fingers are on sale in the markets of the capital city, Brazzaville.

Animals in Danger

During the 1970s, people in Rwanda and Zaïre began selling gorilla hands as souvenirs for **tourists**. Many mountain gorillas were killed to make these souvenirs. The number of mountain gorillas was already low because of **poaching** and the destruction of their habitats. The survival of the whole subspecies was threatened.

Grisly souvenirs: gorilla hands on sale to tourists at a stall in Brazzaville.

Some families of mountain gorillas had been studied for ten years by a famous **primatologist**, Dr Dian Fossey. She had watched one young male gorilla grow up. He was known as 'Digit'.

This is a poster of 'Digit', who was killed by poachers. People were so shocked by his death that they gave money to help to save the mountain gorilla.

Animals in Danger

In 1977, Digit was killed by poachers. People around the world were shocked when they found out what had happened to Digit and to many other mountain gorillas. They gave money to a fund to 'save the mountain gorilla'.

Dian Fossey set up a new charity called the Digit Fund. The money raised is used to pay for extra **patrols** to stop poachers. In 1985, Dian Fossey was murdered. A mystery still surrounds her death. But the Digit Fund is continuing the work she was doing in Rwanda.

This silverback has been injured by a poacher's trap. It has been sent to sleep so that it can be treated by a vet. There are so few mountain gorillas that the survival of every one is important.

Animals in Danger

Many **conservationists** advised the Rwandan government on the best way to protect the gorillas. Several conservation groups decided to work together under a new name – the 'Mountain Gorilla Project' (MGP). They helped to train the guards who worked in Rwanda's **national parks**. They also gave the guards better equipment to help in the fight against the poachers.

Most Rwandan people had never seen a gorilla. They had no national television service and few people were able to go to see a film. The Mountain Gorilla Project visited schools and villages to tell people about the gorillas living in their country. The MGP also explained what could be done to protect the gorillas. This conservation education was very successful. The grisly trade in gorilla souvenirs ended. Now gorillas are very popular in Rwanda. They are shown on banknotes and stamps. A pop song has even been written about them.

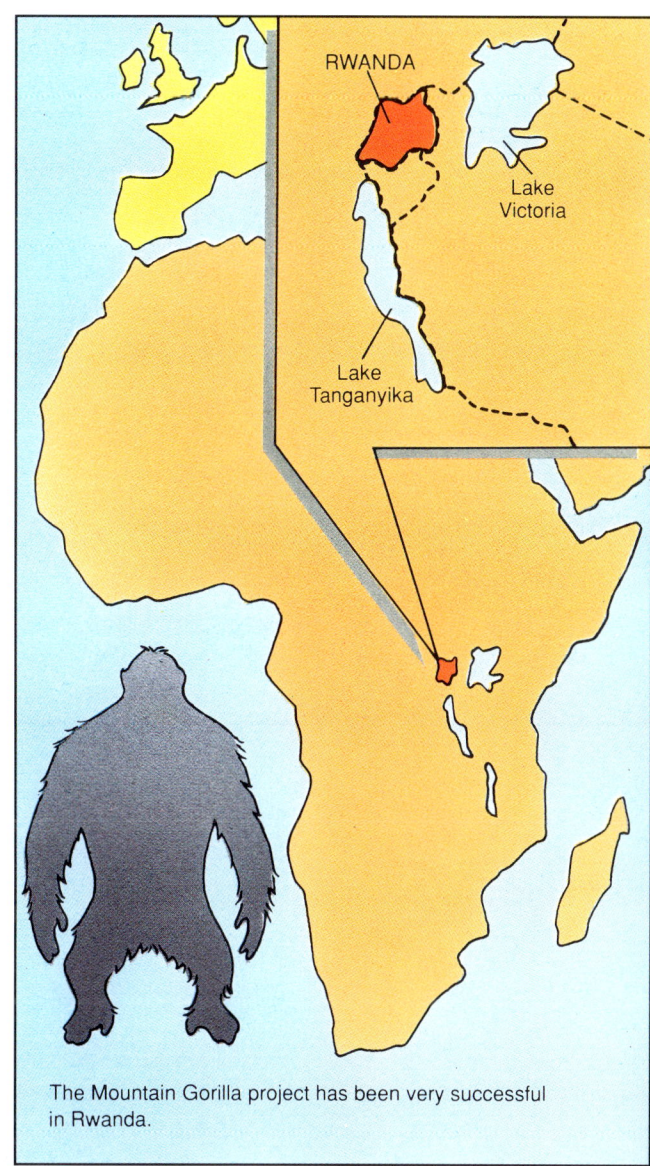

The Mountain Gorilla project has been very successful in Rwanda.

Today the number of mountain gorillas is rising slowly. The work of the MGP is being copied in Zaïre and Uganda. Conservationists hope that similar projects will soon start in west Africa.

Animals in Danger

The food eaten by birds of prey often gets them into trouble. Some eat animals which we use for food. In Australia many farmers believed that Wedge-tailed Eagles killed their lambs and chickens, so they started to kill the eagles. They even offered money rewards (bounties) for dead eagles.

Many were shot, and others were poisoned or trapped and left to die. But when scientists studied Wedge-tailed Eagles, they found that the birds mostly ate rabbits. They only ate lambs that were already dead. Many farmers stopped shooting Wedge-tailed eagles when they were told this.

Gamekeepers hang birds and animals that they have killed from posts called gibbets. This dead Sparrowhawk is hanging from a gamekeeper's gibbet.

Animals in Danger

A Bald Eagle snatches a salmon from an Alaskan river.

In Canada, fishermen believed that Bald Eagles were eating too many salmon, so that there were not enough left for the fishermen. The birds were hunted and even chased and shot from aeroplanes. Over 120,000 birds were killed between 1917 and 1950. Bald Eagles were only saved when they became so rare that the government passed special laws to protect them. People who kill them are now fined or sent to prison.

Birds of prey in many countries are now protected by law. But some people go on killing birds of prey. They still think that the birds do harm to other animals.

Animals in Danger

Pesticides are poisonous chemicals. They are used by farmers to kill insects that attack their crops. But many other animals may be poisoned by pesticides too, because they are part of a **food chain**. For example, a mouse might eat wheat that has been sprayed with pesticides. A Kestrel might then eat the mouse. The poisonous pesticides pass into the Kestrel's body. If the Kestrel eats more mice, it may die, because it has so many poisons in its body.

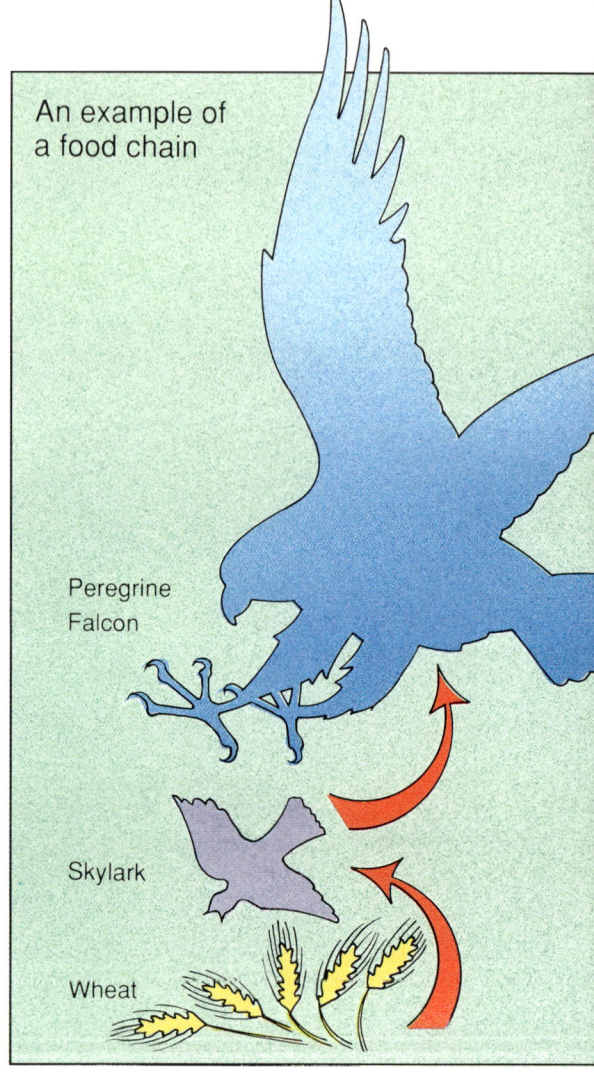

An example of a food chain

Peregrine Falcon

Skylark

Wheat

Pesticides do not always kill birds of prey. Sometimes they just stop the birds breeding properly. The shells of eggs from poisoned birds of prey are so thin that when the female **incubates** them, they smash under her weight.

Kites have become very rare in Britain. These birds, found in Wales, had been poisoned.

Animals in Danger

A Bald Eagle turning the eggs in the nest as it incubates them.

Some eggs do not hatch because the chick inside is dead, killed by the poisons already in its body. If no chicks are hatched, there are no new birds to replace birds which die during the winter. If no new birds are born for a long time, the whole species will eventually die out.

Solving this problem is very difficult. Some countries have now banned the use of certain pesticides. But it takes many years for pesticides to disappear from the soil, and birds of prey are only slowly recovering.

Animals in Danger

The Sparrowhawk hunts by darting along hedges, swooping from one side to the other. If it finds a small bird, it chases it. Many Sparrowhawks are injured or killed when they swoop over hedges by the sides of roads and are hit by cars. Others are hurt when they hunt near houses. They fly into windows as they chase birds from garden bird-tables.

This Sparrowhawk has caught a Great Tit.

This Buzzard had been hit by a car. It recovered in a rehabilitation centre and was released back into the wild.

There are now hospitals for birds, called rehabilitation centres. Injured birds of prey can be taken to them and given time to get better. When they have recovered, they are released back into the wild.

Birds of prey sometimes sit on power lines and pylons, looking out for prey. This can be very dangerous. If the birds touch the wrong parts of the wires, they can be **electrocuted**. In the deserts

Animals in Danger

Bald Eagles perching on a special platform. It stops them from being electrocuted by the power lines that run underneath.

and grasslands of North America several hundred Golden Eagles, Bald Eagles and Red-tailed Hawks are electrocuted each year.

It is easy to stop these accidents by putting safe perches and nest platforms on the poles and changing the patterns of the wires. When scientists explained this, many power companies changed their poles. Now fewer birds of prey are killed.

Animals in Danger

Brown bears were once quite common in northern countries of the world. However, in Europe these bears are now very **rare** because so many were killed by people in the past. In Scandinavia and eastern Europe all together a few thousand bears survive, but in Spain only about thirty are left.

In Canada, Alaska, and the northern USSR, there are still many brown bears. This is because these countries still have large areas of land without people. North American people call brown bears 'grizzlies'. In the rest of the USA there are 1,000 grizzlies left: in 1800, there were over 100,000 grizzlies.

The grizzly's main problem is that it breeds very slowly. A female might have as many as three cubs at one time.

Brown bear (also called Grizzly bear)

Scientific name: *Ursus arctos* (European brown bear)
Ursus horribilis (Grizzly bear)

Length head to tail: 2.0 – 2.8 m.

Weight: female 80 – 205 kg; male up to 440 kg.

Distribution: Many bears still live in Arctic Canada and Alaska. 1,000 left in rest of USA. Several thousand brown bears survive in USSR and eastern Europe. A few hundred bears left in Norway and Sweden; only about thirty left in Spain.

Habitat: forest and open grasslands.

Animals in Danger

She must look after them until they are three or even four years old. She only starts a new family when her young can look after themselves. This means that when people started to kill grizzlies in large numbers, not enough new bears were born to replace those that were killed.

There are still some brown bears left in Scandinavian forests. This one was photographed in Sweden.

Grizzly bears are at risk because people are destroying their habitat. In many places, the woods and meadows grizzlies live in have been turned into farmland.

Many North American forests have been cut down for timber or cleared for farmland. Grizzlies like to live in these wild forests.

Animals in Danger

In North America many people dislike grizzlies because they raid rubbish dumps and even occasionally kill farmers' calves. The main cause of death for grizzly bears is hunting for sport. People feel very brave if they can kill a grizzly bear because they think it is a frightening animal.

It is not hard to understand why people are afraid of grizzlies. A full-grown bear weighs half a tonne. It is very strong and can charge at 50 kph.

Cruel traps like this were once used to catch and injure bears. Now these traps are against the law.

A notice in Yellowstone National Park, USA, warns campers to take care when bears are around.

Animals in Danger

In Denali National Park, Alaska, bears are protected. Lucky visitors sometimes see grizzlies sleeping in the daytime.

However, people can walk about in bear country without being harmed, if they behave in the right way. In Denali National Park, Alaska, grizzly bears are very common. Everyone who visits Denali is taught what to do when they arrive. If people camp there, they must keep all food in boxes which the bears cannot open. When the visitors walk, they must sing or clap their hands. Some people wear bells which ring as they walk. All these things let the bears know that people are coming. Then the grizzlies are not taken by surprise and alarmed into attacking someone. Although people have come very close to grizzlies in Denali, no one has ever been badly hurt.

Animals in Danger

Inuit have been hunting polar bears with spears for hundreds of years. They eat the meat and use the bear's furry skin to make warm blankets. Polar bears are not in danger from the Inuit hunters because they only kill small numbers. However, when Europeans came to the Arctic, they wanted to sell polar bear skins. They paid the Inuit to kill many bears, and before long polar bears were rare in some parts of the Arctic.

An Inuit man skins a polar bear he has hunted. He is wearing trousers made of polar bear fur.

Animals in Danger

In the early 1970s wildlife workers decided that too many polar bears were being killed. In 1973 the Arctic countries (USSR, Canada, USA, Greenland and Norway) agreed to hunt fewer bears. Today, no more than a thousand bears are killed each year, mostly by Inuit and other traditional hunters. Now that the bears are better protected, they are no longer in danger.

Now that they are protected by people, polar bears face a brighter future.

Polar bears are bred in zoos all over the world but they cannot enjoy life as much as wild polar bears.

Whales in danger

Animals in Danger

Three hundred years ago the oceans of the world were teeming with whales. An early whaler who visited the Arctic said that it would be possible to walk from his ship to the shore on the backs of whales. Now human activities have threatened the survival of many species of whales and dolphins.

The history of whaling is a sad story of humans' greed. The whalers hunted one species after another until there were almost no whales left. The first whales to be hunted were slow-moving and floated when dead. They were named right whales (as

A minke whale is winched on board a whaling ship.

Animals in Danger

A huge sperm whale at a whaling station in the Azores, where these whales used to be hunted for their oil.

they were the right whales to catch). The Atlantic **populations** of right whales almost became **extinct** two hundred years ago. Next to suffer was the sperm whale, which was hunted for its oil.

In 1860 whalers began to use harpoon guns, which made it easier to catch some of the faster baleen whales. As whales became more scarce in the North, the whalers moved to the Antarctic. At first, humpback whales were caught. Next to follow was the blue whale. By 1931 few blue whales were left, so the whalers began to catch fin whales. Now the only whale left in sufficiently large numbers to be worth chasing is the 9 metre-long minke whale.

Animals in Danger

Many poisonous chemicals leak into rivers and find their way to the sea. Thirty years ago **pesticides** such as DDT were widely used. DDT does not break down naturally. Now we realize how dangerous DDT is and it is no longer used.

PCBs have also been dumped in the seas. These are very poisonous chemicals used in the manufacture of plastics and electrical equipment. Once in the sea, PCBs and DDT can pass into the bodies of marine mammals, including cetaceans. These poisons build up in their bodies and can be passed on from a mother to her calf in her milk.

The beluga, or white whale, may be the most polluted mammal on earth. The bodies of dead belugas often contain very high levels of dangerous chemicals such as PCBs.

Animals in Danger

Like other cetaceans, common dolphins may be harmed by the many poisonous chemicals that are dumped in the sea.

With so many **pollutants** in the seas, whales and dolphins often absorb several different chemicals in their bodies. Scientists can measure the levels of chemicals found in the bodies of dead cetaceans. However, it is difficult for us to find out what happens to the living animal when these chemicals mix together in its body. Recently scientists have found out how some chemicals have harmed seals. They may lower an animal's resistance to disease. Also, they can reduce the seals' breeding success.

The world's oceans are littered with rubbish, such as discarded plastic bags. Whales and dolphins often swallow this rubbish, and their guts can become choked with pieces of plastic.

Animals in Danger

Whales and dolphins are sometimes unpopular with fishermen. In some countries they are blamed for eating too much fish. In Japan many thousands of dolphins have been killed for this reason. However, the real problem is overfishing by people.

All around the world, whales and dolphins are dying because they become entangled in nylon fishing nets. These strong synthetic fibre nets are becoming more widely used because they are inexpensive.

Drift nets are also very dangerous. They are used at night and are almost invisible in the water. Drift nets may be 70 km long and will catch anything. Whales, dolphins, seabirds and turtles are often trapped and killed. Japan and Korea use drift nets a great deal in all the world's oceans. Many countries are trying to stop them doing this.

A Hector's dolphin entangled in a fishing net off the coast of New Zealand. Cetaceans often drown when caught in nets.

Animals in Danger

The dolphins in this Sri Lankan fish market have been caught accidentally in nets. Some 40,000 dolphins drown in Sri Lankan fishing nets every year.

In one area of the Pacific Ocean, dolphins and yellow-finned tuna swim together. Tuna fishermen use the schools of dolphins to find the tuna. A speed boat is used to set a long net around the school of fish, and the tuna fish and dolphins are caught together. In the last thirty years, seven million dolphins have died in this way. There are other ways of catching tuna that do not harm dolphins. One way is by using hooks and lines.

Elephants in danger

Animals in Danger

Elephants once lived in many parts of Africa and southern Asia. They had an important effect on their surroundings. When there was no rain for a long time, elephants dug for water with their tusks. They pushed over small trees to feed on nuts and leaves. They even helped to make new forests grow, because they passed tree seeds in their droppings. This made their habitat better for them to live in, and better for the other animals that lived there too, including humans.

Elephants dig in earth to find salt to eat.

As people take more land to build homes, the elephant's habitats are destroyed.

Today, the areas where elephants live have become much fewer. In many places, their habitat is being destroyed. The elephants need trees and grass for food but humans also need land so that they can grow crops for food. As the number of humans grows, they need more land to grow crops. They take over the land that the elephants used to live on.

Animals in Danger

Elephants love to play in water. Sometimes they go under water and use their trunks as snorkels.

What an elephant needs

- **Food** – elephants eat 150-225 kg of fresh greens, roots, bark, buds and fruit each day.
- **Water** – an adult elephant drinks more than 200 litres per day, and likes to bathe to keep cool and moist.
- **Mud** – elephants plaster on mud to prevent sunburn and bites from flies.
- **Salt** – elephants need salt to live. They cannot lick salt from rocks as other animals do, so they use their tusks to break off lumps of salt rock to eat.
- **Space** – an elephant may need as much as 3,000 sq km of land.

Animals in Danger

No one knows exactly how many elephants there are in the world. Scientists need to find out how many there are, so that they can work out the best way to protect elephants. Elephants that live on the savannah can usually be seen from an aeroplane. It is quite easy to count them. But they stand in the shade of trees during the hottest part of the day, trying to keep cool. Then they cannot be seen from an aeroplane. They are hidden by the trees.

Elephants standing under a tree in the savannah. They are trying to find shelter from the midday sun.

Animals in Danger

Rangers work out how many elephants live in an area by counting piles of dung.

Elephants living in forests cannot be counted from an aeroplane at all. Cars and trucks cannot be driven through the thick forest, so the only way to count the elephants is on foot.

Counting elephants in this way sounds like very dangerous work. Sometimes the trees and bushes are so thick that you can only see a little way ahead. You never know whether a large animal is going to be around the next bend in the path. But the people counting the elephants do not try to find and count every herd. Instead, they walk in a straight line through the forest and count all the piles of dung that they see. Then they can estimate how many elephants are living nearby.

There are four forest elephants in this picture. Can you see them all?

Animals in Danger

Although it is very difficult to count living elephants, we can work out how many elephants have been killed. Many elephants are killed every year because people want the **ivory** that their tusks are made from. By counting the number of tusks that have been sold, scientists can work out how many elephants have been killed.

Even female elephants, with their slender tusks, are killed by ivory poachers.

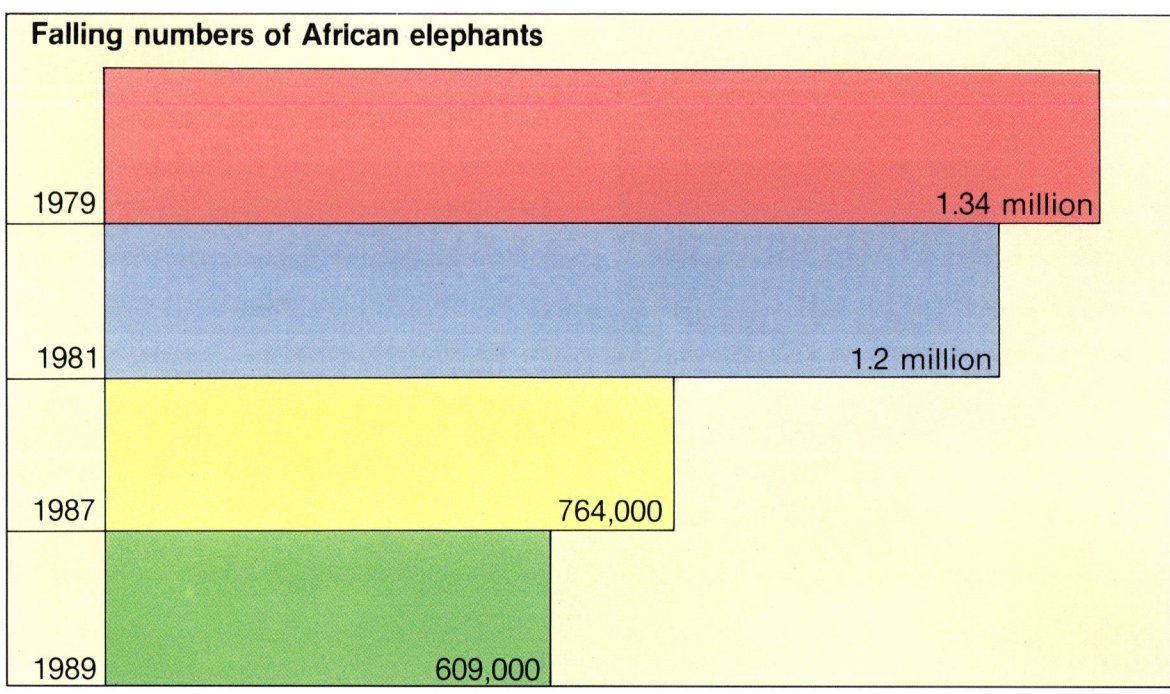

Falling numbers of African elephants

- 1979: 1.34 million
- 1981: 1.2 million
- 1987: 764,000
- 1989: 609,000

Animals in Danger

An elephant's jaw-bone. In many parts of Africa, there are more dead elephants than living ones.

In some places, there may be too many elephants living in a small area. This usually happens because elephants have come to live in a **national park** or **reserve**, where they are protected by the **rangers**. In most parts of Africa, elephant numbers have fallen very quickly. They are remaining at the same level, or growing, in only South Africa, Zimbabwe, Botswana, Malawi and Namibia. If the number of elephants continues to fall as quickly as it did in the early 1980s, the African elephant will become **extinct** in the wild in less than twenty years.

Animals in Danger

An Asian elephant enjoying a shower. African and Asian elephants are now on the list of endangered species.

In 1989, **conservationists** from 103 countries met to decide the best way of protecting the African elephant and how to control the ivory trade. They decided that the African elephant should have the same protection as the Asian elephant. People are no longer allowed to send ivory from Africa to be sold in other countries. But ivory poaching may continue, because some countries do not agree that the ivory trade should be banned. The ivory trade will only stop when people refuse to buy ivory. If you see ivory carvings or jewellery, remember that an elephant has been killed to make them.

Animals in Danger

Many schoolchildren in African countries join clubs to find out more about wildlife. The clubs are based on the Wildlife Clubs of Kenya which were set up more than twenty years ago. The children go to talks, films and slide shows about wildlife. Sometimes, they go on a field trip into a national park or reserve to watch the animals.

Many of the people who now work in Kenya's national parks were in the Wildlife Club when they were at school. They are interested in wildlife and are working to protect the animals and their habitats. With the help of people like these, there may be a better future for elephants, and all wildlife, throughout Asia and Africa.

The future of Africa's elephants, and of all the world's wildlife, lies in our hands.

Why are rhinos at risk?

Animals in Danger

In Far Eastern countries, especially China, people believe that rhinos can be used in medicines. The horn is supposed to be a good cure for sore throats, fevers, bad backs, stiff joints and other illnesses.

Pieces of a rhino's skin, its toenails, and even its blood and dung are also used as medicine, but the horn is always said to be the best.

Rich people will pay a lot of money for quite small pieces of rhino horn. To obtain a rhino's horn, hunters have to kill the animal.

The rhinos in Asia have been hunted for hundreds of years for their horns. This is the main reason why the Indian, Javan and Sumatran rhinos are so rare. Now the Asian people use the horn of African rhinos for medicine.

*Horns taken from black and white rhinos (**above**) are sliced and used as medicines in China (**right**).*

Animals in Danger

In North Yemen, the boys are given a special dagger when they become men. The most expensive daggers have a handle carved from rhino horn. North Yemen is a very rich country because the people there sell oil all over the world. Many Yemeni people can afford to buy very expensive daggers to give to their sons.

The dagger handles used to be made from the horns of white rhinos. Then they became too rare for the hunters to find, so they hunted black rhinos instead. Now black rhinos are hard to find in most African countries.

The custom of making dagger handles from rhino horn is not as common as it was. The richest people still buy them, though, and so the hunting goes on.

The dagger worn by this Yemeni man has a carved rhino-horn handle.

Animals in Danger

The people who make rhino horn daggers or medicines for the Far East do not hunt the rhinos themselves. Instead, they pay poachers in Africa to go out and kill rhinos. They hunt animals even though it is against the law.

Many of the African rhino poachers come from Zambia. There are almost no rhinos left in Zambia, so the poachers cross the River Zambesi in boats to get to Zimbabwe. There are still quite a lot of rhinos left in Zimbabwe. On the other side of the river, guards wait for the poachers to arrive. They try to catch them, to stop them killing the rhinos. Often the poachers shoot at

A collection of rhino horns that were taken by poachers. To get the horns, the poachers had to kill many rhinos.

Animals in Danger

An armed guard watches over a white rhino in Meru National Park, Kenya.

them, and some guards have been killed. Many poachers have been killed also.

If the poachers can find a rhino, they shoot it. They chop off the horn and try to get back to the river. Sometimes the guards catch them on the way back. However, by then it is too late, because the rhino is dead.

In 1970, there were 19,000 black rhinos in Kenya. Now only 100 black rhinos survive. In 1984, there were about 8,000 black rhinos in all of Africa. Now there may be less than 2,000 left.

Animals in Danger

By 1960 the white rhino had been hunted until it was very **rare** in South Africa. People collected up all the white rhinos they could find. Some of them were taken to Whipsnade Zoo in England. The rest were moved to a safe place in an African national park, where guards protect them. Both groups of rhinos produced babies, and now the white rhino is safe.

These men are fitting a radio transmitter to a white rhino which has been put to sleep. The radio signals will help guards to keep track of the rhino.

Animals in Danger

This black rhino has been moved out of danger into a national park in southern Africa. Guards are releasing the rhino into its safe new home.

In Kenya and Zimbabwe people are trying to protect the black rhino. First, they buy an area of land and build a strong fence around it, to keep the poachers out and the rhinos in. Then they catch the rhinos. They take them in lorries to their new home and let them go. They hope that the rhinos will breed. Many **conservation organizations**, like WWF and Zoo Check, are giving money and help to support projects like these.

One day wildlife workers hope to release the protected black and white rhinos into the wild again. However, this can only happen if poaching stops. If nobody buys rhino horn, no one will pay the poachers and then they will not go on hunting rhinos.

Why are pandas so rare?

Animals in Danger

Giant pandas have probably never been common anywhere. There are several reasons for this. They do not produce many babies. They can only live in cool bamboo forests. Each panda needs a big area of forest to itself, and even large areas of suitable mountain forest only have room for a few pandas.

These are the mountain forests of Sichuan where pandas live. In such dense forests, pandas rarely meet.

Animals in Danger

Pandas also need plenty of their favourite bamboo. This plant has a very unusual way of growing. For perhaps a hundred years, bamboo plants spread by underground branches. Then suddenly, all the bamboo plants over a wide area flower, make seeds and die. This leaves no food for the pandas until new plants grow from the seeds. Many pandas die of **starvation** when this happens, as it did in 1975–6.

A bamboo grove provides plenty of food for a hungry panda.

The forests of Sichuan are being cut down to make room for villages and provide land for crops.

For thousands of years, the giant panda's homeland in south-west China was very hard for people to reach, so it was left undisturbed for pandas and other wildlife. Now the millions of Chinese people need more land for their farms and villages. Modern roads help them to reach even the furthest mountains of Sichuan. As the people cut down the mountain forests, the pandas have fewer unspoiled bamboo groves to live in.

Animals in Danger

Pandas are always popular in zoos. Here Chia-Chia at London Zoo is visited by three Chinese children.

Another reason why pandas are rare is that people have captured them from the wild. Since pandas were first brought out of China, zoos around the world have wanted to have their own pandas to attract crowds of visitors. In the past expensive **expeditions** were sent to China to catch and bring back wild pandas. Fortunately those days are now over. The People's Republic of China banned the hunting of pandas in 1962. Now zoos can only obtain pandas as a gift from the Chinese people or from other zoos.

Animals in Danger

However, panda-hunting still goes on in spite of the ban. The pandas are not captured to be taken to zoos but are killed for their skins. Panda fur is too coarse to use for fur coats but some people like to have a panda skin to decorate their home. In Japan people will pay a great deal (over £120,000) to have a black and white panda skin rug on the floor.

Of course, this hunting is against the law and if the hunters are caught they are imprisoned for life, or even sentenced to death. However, the hunters still manage to smuggle a few panda skins out of China. They take the risk because they are well paid by the people who want the panda skins.

The giant panda's fur is too coarse to make coats but is sometimes used to make rugs.

Animals in Danger

Although pandas are in danger from hunting, the main threat to them is the loss of their bamboo forests. There is some good news for pandas, however. The Chinese people and international conservation organizations are working hard to protect them.

Now there are twelve special panda **reserves** in China, where some 450 pandas are living in safety.

Above *There is plenty of bamboo growing in the panda reserves.*

Left *These Chinese workers are moving a panda to an area within a reserve, where it can live in safety.*

Animals in Danger

The Wolong Research and Conservation Centre. You can see cages where pandas are kept while scientists study them.

The reserves were created to protect the pandas and the bamboo forests they need. The cutting down of bamboo and felling of trees by people is strictly controlled. Armed guards patrol the reserves to protect the pandas from hunters and to ensure that local people do not destroy the trees.

As well as protecting the pandas, it is important to tell the local people why these animals are so special. So the people from 5,000 villages in Sichuan are taught about the need to protect pandas and how to care for starving pandas. They are told why they should not cut down trees and bamboo. If a panda causes damage to the local people's farm crops, the people are paid to cover the damage.

The largest reserve, at Wolong, was created in 1975. In 1980 the Chinese government and WWF built a special panda-breeding and research centre there.

Animals in Danger

charm An object that some people believe can give magical protection from danger or illness.
conservationists People who work to protect animals and plants.
conservation organization A group of people who work to protect animals, plants, and the places they live in.
electrocuted Killed by an electric shock.
expedition A journey to a distant country made by a team of people.
extinct When the last member of a particular species has died. The dinosaurs are extinct, for example.
food chain A series of animals which depend on each other for food. For example, a blue tit might eat an insect. The blue tit might be eaten by a sparrowhawk.
habitat The natural home of any animal or plant. For example, it can be a forest, field or stream.
incubates Keeps eggs warm by sitting on them.
ivory The material that an elephant's tusks are made from.
national parks Areas of land that are left wild and protected by the government. Many animals can live more safely in national parks.
patrol A group of people who work in the national park making sure that the wildlife is safe.
pesticides Harmful chemicals often used by farmers to kill pests that eat their crops.
poaching Hunting that is against the law. People who do this are called poachers.
pollutant A poisonous chemical released into the environment by humans.
population The number of animals belonging to a particular species found in a certain area.
primatologist A scientist who studies primates.
rangers People who work in a national park or reserve and protect its wildlife.
rare Very few in number.
reserve An area of land where wildlife is protected.
starvation Having too little food to survive.
timber companies Groups of people who cut down trees to sell. The trees are used for building and for making expensive furniture.
tourists People who are visiting a place as part of their holiday.

Animals in Danger

Africa 17–21, 40, 45, 47, 50, 51
Alaska 28, 31
Antarctic 35
Arctic 32–34
Asia 8, 40, 46, 47
Australia 22

Bald eagle 23, 25, 27
bamboo 55
bears 28–33
   breeding 28
   cubs 28
   food 29
   habitat 29
   protecting 33
Beluga whale 36
birds of prey 22–27
   breeding 24
   hunting 22, 23
black rhino 51, 53
blue whale 35
Britain 24
brown bear 28–31
buzzard 26

Canada 28, 33
cattle 11, 13
cetaceans 36, 37
China 48, 55
Congo 18, 19
conservationists 21, 46

deer 14
Digit Fund 20
dolphins 34–39

elephants 40–47
   African 45–47
   Asian 46
   cow 44
   habitat 40–43
   herds 43
   rangers 45
   reserves 45, 47
   tusks 44
Europe 28
extinction
   of tigers 11, 12
   of whales 35

farming 10, 13–16, 29, 55, 59
finwhale 35
fishing 38, 39
forests 29, 43
   destruction of 10, 11, 54, 55

forest elephant 43
Fossey, Dian 19, 20

golden eagle 27
gorillas 15–21
   as food 17
   charms 18
   food 16
   habitat 15, 16, 18
   home range 15–17
   hunting 17
   males 19
   patrols 20
   subspecies of 16, 19–21
   silverback 16, 20
   tourism 17
Greenland 33
grizzly bear 28–31

humpback whale 35

India 9, 14, 53
Indian rhino 48, 53
Indonesia 14
Inuit 32, 33
ivory 44, 46

Japan 38, 57
Javan rhino 48

Kenya 47, 51, 53
kestrel 24
kite 24

Malawi 45
minke whale 34, 35
mountain gorilla 16, 19, 20
Mountain Gorilla Project 21

Namibia 45
national parks 21, 31, 45, 47, 52, 53
Nepal 53
New Zealand 38
Norway 28, 33

oceans, pollution of 36, 37
Operation Tiger 14

pandas 54–59
   hunting 56, 57
   protecting 58
   reserves 58, 59
   trade in skins 57
PCBs 36
pesticides 24, 25, 36

poaching
   gorilla 17, 19–21
   rhino 50, 51, 53
polar bear 32, 33

red-tailed hawk 27
rhinos 48–53
   conservation 53
   guards 50–52
   horns 48–53
   hunting of 49–51
   protecting 52, 53
right whale 34, 35
Rwanda 19–21

savannah 42
Scandinavia 28
seals 37
South Africa 45, 52
South-east Asia 10
Spain 28
sparrowhawk 22, 26
sperm whale 35
Sumatran rhino 48
Sweden 28, 29

tigers 8–14
   food 8
   hunting 8, 9, 11
   Indian 12
   reserves 12–14
   Siberian 13
   Sumatran 8
   territory 8
tropical rainforest 15, 18
tuna fish 39

USA 27, 28, 30, 33
USSR 28, 33

wedge-tailed eagle 22
whales 34–39
whaling 34, 35
wild boar 14
Wildlife Clubs 47
wildlife workers 33
Wolong reserve 59
World Wide Fund for Nature 59

Yemen 49

Zaire 19, 21
Zambia 50
Zimbabwe 45, 53
zoos 13, 33, 52, 53, 56